Homeschooling In Times of Covid-19

KAREN WHITE PORTER

DR. MARTHA JOSEPH WATTS

Edited by Patricia Ashton

And

Mary Bahr

DEDICATION

To Cole and all the children who will be
homeschooled

CONTENTS

K .W. Porter and M. J. Watts

ACKNOWLEDGMENTS

A special thanks to the editors Mary Bahr, Pat Ashton, Jenifer Dearinger, Barbara Bockman, and Dr. Nancy Perry. To all the supporters Nurseen Davis, Anthony Drigo, Muriel Baptiste, James Porter, Cole Porter, Francis Joseph, Francisca John Baptiste, and other family members. To the parents Ken and Narissa Gallik, Melanie, and Doug Devonald-batt, Alicia Lipham, and Kurt Mauser, Jessica Isaac, Susan Litel, and others, To the Devonald-Batt family, the Lipham family, the Woolsey Family, the Isaac Family, and others who have entrusted us to teach and evaluate their children. To the students, Lacy, Mark, Daniel, Elizabeth, Alexander, Kathrine, Nicholas, Katie, Robert, Lars, Cicily, Macey, Liam, Artur, Kyngielle, Angelica, Frazier, Ossyriah, Alethia, Skylar, Erick, Erin, and others.

Chapter 1
Why Homeschool?

Parents have come to me over the years to ask for advice on how to homeschool their child because I was a teacher and I have homeschooled my daughter. You are reading this book because you are thinking of taking full responsibility for your child's education in your own home for all or part of this year. Do not panic. You can do this. I have helped many parents do this with great success and you can do it too. The requirements are not beyond your ability. For some states, it is purely a matter of filling out a letter of intention and providing a crate filled with your child's work that a certified teacher evaluates at the end of the year. This book tells you what to do, and how to do it. Research shows an involved parent makes an advanced student. You do not need to be an expert in any topic so long as you have the answer key, and your attention to meaningful instruction for your child. So, let us begin. You may feel the options before you during this pandemic are not what your child needs at this time, and you want the best for your child. I have teamed up with other educators to provide you with the best possible homeschooling guide.

As teacher, I have learned no one educational approach fits all children. I built my own system for tailoring an education for the individual needs of children. I hope to share this system with you for your attempts at homeschooling. The curriculum and teaching approaches that I am familiar with may help you decide if private homeschooling is for you. I have taught hundreds of children and adults. But, most importantly, I homeschooled my own daughter for three years.

Homeschooling in Times of COVID-19

Parents who do not feel safe putting children in local schools during times of uncertainty will choose to homeschool. They may not ordinarily choose to homeschool, but they are being forced to because of the COVID-19 pandemic. Whether it is because of health or safety reasons or for quality concerns, I have always felt their reasons are justified, and they should be given the needed information to choose options for their child's education. With my advice, parents have been able to keep up with the State Standards, and maintain a home education that enables them to return to the public school when they feel confident that it will be in their best interests to do so.

The response by government and school boards to the 2020 pandemic has been a hodgepodge of policies that are confusing and even dangerous in some instances and have many parents genuinely concerned. For this reason, I have prepared a step by step process to homeschool until you feel safe to return. In the meantime, remember there is so much the public-school system has to offer families. We should honor the efforts school boards, teachers, and principals are taking at this time to help children in these difficult times. They are true heroes.

There are several reasons why you may be considering homeschooling. Perhaps your town, state, or nation is in turmoil and unable to give you a reasonable sense of how your school will keep your children safe and provide them a quality education. You may see pandemic guidelines being disregarded, and you do not want to put your children's life or educational future at stake. You may worry that your child will get an endless barrage of untrained substitute teachers because older well-seasoned teachers do not want to risk their lives getting infected with the virus.

Homeschool can remedy many of these issues and avoid a one size fits all approach to teaching or learning. If you have some of these concerns, the resources to stay home, and you do not feel safe sending your child to a brick and mortar building, this is the time to try homeschooling. Children in grades K-8, can do this with little change to their educational plan or trajectory. Older students are often capable of independent learning and some can successfully take online courses such as FLVS if you are in Florida. Go to https://www.flvs.net/ or your state's Department of Education's virtual school website.

Locate the benchmarks and standards that are required to learn for each grade level. Check to see if your local school district has tips and guidelines to help support the social and emotional needs of your child. The responsibility to weigh choices and decide what is in the best interests of a child belongs to the parent, not the government.

After the decision to homeschool a child is made, please move forward with honesty, integrity, and support for the educators on the front line. Let the officials know you are homeschooling. Ask the administrators to let you know what kind of support they can provide for you. Contact your local school board's homeschooling liaison for up to date information. Keep in touch with the teacher your child would have been assigned to. You may even be able to coordinate with the classroom's assigned educator. We are all in this together.

If you follow these simple instructions,

you can do it. I am offering you a recipe like baking a cake that makes it easy to transition your child from public school to homeschooling. What I am providing can be done with or without internet. In addition, a single schedule for all siblings will provide ways to adapt with multiple children so you do not have to worry about sharing the internet access or multiple devices. An example of what a routine schedule should look like is below. Regardless of what time you begin your day, be consistent. Please refer to this sample when setting up your own classroom.

Mon	Tue	Wed	Thur	Fri	Time
Math	Project learning	Math	Project learning	Math	9:00
Play	Play	Play	Play	Play	10:00
Lang Arts	Lang Arts	Project learning	Lang Arts	Project learning	11:00
History	Science	History	Science	History	1:00
Play	Play	Play	Play	Play	2:00
Art	PE	Music	PE	Art	3:00

Daily Schedule Sample

Chapter 2
Your Child's Needs, Interests, and Goals

A four-step personalized process will motivate your child to participate in society in positive ways. Start your education journal now.

1. Set goals that your child can achieve within the scope of a year.

2. Find what goals your child wants to reach.

3. Develop rules and structure to achieve goals.

4. Record when your child reaches the goals.

This process will make your child a

stakeholder in their educational plan.

Setting Goals

Allow your child to set a goal to accomplish by the end of the year. Also include intermediate goals. This is very empowering for your child. You might be surprised with what your child comes up with. It gives them ownership and they become accountable. Write a sentence such as, "By the end of the year I want to learn how to swim.", or "I want to draw or paint 12 drawings of horses." Or, "I want to read the entire *Diary of a Wimpy Kid series*." You can be more formulaic about it and have them write down a sentence such as: This year I plan to _____... I will do this by _____, and _____ at _____ with _____ and _____." All in all, the goals need to be realistic, doable activities that allow for choice. Only then will they have a sense of satisfaction in their own achievements.

Finding Goals

Finding the goals your child wants to

10

achieve can be eye-opening. If you use the interest inventories provided here, you may find your child will have ideas about what to do which you were unaware. For younger children, read the list with them and let them discuss and circle their interests. Feel free to add items to the inventory list if something is missing that they want to do. These essential lists to read with your child are divided by younger elementary, older elementary, middle school, and high school. Often children do not fit into one of these "educational levels." I have worked with many children who are younger elementary in math but older elementary or even middle or high school in reading or science. You should select what works best for your child. Read all the lists with them or if you wish, make up your own. After going over these lists, you will find charts with more detailed suggestions for creating goals or with activities to fulfill goals - you can read or share these with your child.

After you complete the interest inventory, discuss what your child circled and how your family could accomplish these activities or possible alternatives. You may need to take a break from this exercise for reflection time. Later, or the next day work with your child to make a list of the circled items in order of preference and include how feasible each item might be. Some choices may be limited by season or time. Others may be limited by money or location or available supplies. At the end of this task, your child will have options to pick from to make goals that will be written down and kept in their educational journal for the end of year assessment. See interest inventory charts below. These Interest inventories can be used to gauge your child's interests. After that are a set of charts that will show you how to apply your findings.

Interest Inventory: Younger Elementary K-2(3)				
Copyright © 2020 Everfield Press				
Horses Zebras	Volcanoes Explosions	My Body Systems	Piano or Keyboard	Ball Games
Dinosaurs	Stars & Planets	Costumes & Masks	Music	Racing Cars
Snakes & Lizards	Gems & Rocks	Clay & Pottery	Baking & Measuring	Outside games
Vegetable Gardening	Caves & Sinkholes	learn new language	Bells or Xylophone	Dancing
Kangaroo & Koalas	Waterfalls & Rivers Deer	Counting things Puzzles	Museums Monument Heroes	Rainbow Sunlight
Aquarium	Riddles	Fruits	Skating	BINGO
Birds	Comets	Painting	Fashion	Boats
Bears	Beads	Stencils	Stickers	Recycle
Pets – big and little	Mountains & glaciers	Frogs Toads	Model making	Water Safety
Farm Animals	Training animals	Secret Codes	Holidays & decoration	Seasons
African Animals	Matter Atoms & Elements	Cards, Bows & Gift Wrap	Colored chalks or pastels	Helping others
Whales Dolphins	Magnifiers Microscope use	Wishing wells	Fairies & Fairy Tales	Knights Castles

Interest Inventory: Younger Elementary 3-5(6)
Copyright © 2020 Everfield Press

Black Hole Big Bang	Archaeology Early human	Native American	Light & Lenses	Scary Tales
Extreme Weather	Chemical Experiment	Famous Artists	Sand Painting	Ping Pong
Meteor Showers	Prehistoric Creatures	Famous Singers	Mosaics & Murals	Logic Puzzles
Fossils & Tar Pits	Plates & Continents	Simple Machines	Rock Climbing	Clocks Watches
Rockets & Astronauts	Navigation North Star	Geologic Time Line	Learn new language	Poetry Rhyme
Climates	Explorers	Maps	Greeks	Jokes
Habitats	Social Justice	Inventors	Metrics	Plays
Life Cycles	Amphibians	Trains	Romans	Flute
Animal Tracks	Walking Fish Lung Fish	Leaf Color Change	Natural Pigments	Olympic Games
Things that Fly	Atmosphere Layers	Ocean Layers	Witches & Wizards	Drums Cymbals
State Flowers	Wolves to Dogs	Identify Plants	Mysteries & Clues	Song Writing
State Birds	Shells	Airplanes	Quilting	Cooking
State Reptiles	String Instruments	Scrap Booking	Butter & Cheese	Paper Making

Interest Inventory: Middle School 6-8(9)

Copyright © 2020 Everfield Press

Mechanics	Metaphysics	Ethics	Nonfiction	Bowling
Elements Compound Molecules Reactions	Female/Male animals words (Cow, bull, calf)	Energy Sugar Electricit y E = MC²	Spinning & Weaving Silk, wool Textiles	Robots Drones AI Siri Alexa
Butterfly Garden	Antlers vs. Horns	Time Zones	Acid vs. Base - pH	Board Games
Conduct vs Insulate	Poisonous vs Venomous	Oregon Trail	Musical Segue	Aikido Karate
Nutrition Vitamins Minerals	Magnetism Levitation Auroras	Fungi & Real Zombies	Newton's Laws of Motion	Cooking Business Chef
Buoyancy Density	Disease Incubation	Glass Blowing	Math Magic	Screen Printing
Global Warming Ozone	Collective Terms –herd swarm, pod	Learn a new language	Knots & Rope Making	Anime Cartoon
Industrial Revolution	Language of Flowers	Quantum Theory	Banking & Commerce	Bag Pipes
Anatomy	Photography	Vaccines	Marxism	Yoga
Metals	Flower Parts	Slang	Orchestra	Zodiac
Crystals	Gymnastics	Wars	Folklore	Golf
Gravity	Renaissance	Language	Surrealism	Tie-dye
Zoology	Taxonomy	Utopias	Medicine	Sumi-e

Interest Inventory: High School 9-12
Copyright © 2020 Everfield Press

Microbes	Astronomy	Archery	Advertise	Jazz
Organic Chemistry	Democracy & Freedom	Design & Construct	How to Escape	Folk Songs
Rube Goldberg	Famous Females	Marbling Methods	Measuring Geometry	Solar Power
Physics	Psychology	Grammar	Meditation	Hockey
Forensic Science	Restaurant Management	Codes & Ciphers	Ferment Beer/Wine	Famous Battles
Ecology	Shakespeare	Cities	Justice	Portraits
Parasites	Philosophy	Slavery	First Aid	Fishing
new languages	Probability Games	Hunt/Skin /Tan/hides	Illusions & Tricks	Age of Piracy
Arson Fire Fighting	Presentation Design	Bird Watching	Ballroom Dancing	Marine Biology
Sharks	Calligraphy	Knitting	Idioms	Skiing
Pinhole Camera / Projector	Cosmetology Nails & Hair Styling	Finance Managing Money	Greek & Latin roots & Prefixes	Cars SUVs Trucks
Cake & Cookie Decorating	Wildlife Habitat Management	World Cultures Religions	Human Relations Romance	Support A Cause Protest
Debate	Life Guard	Sailing	Travel	Pilot
Camping	Mythology	Voting	Biking	Fashion

Examples of How to Translate Interests into Goals

Build toys or models from different materials following written instructions	**Figure** why we get sick and how to stay well. Gather supplies that would help	**Illustrate** a poem, or story -use paint, colored pencils or cut up pictures. for book cover	**Count** to make inventories (toys, art supplies, clothes, shoes, food,)
Learn how things grow and stay alive. Plant something or care for a pet	**Write** letters and cards to people who are ill. Try to make them smile.	**Work** with my hands to make clay objects or pottery to display or use.	**Learn** /use a calculator to work with numbers / use measuring for recipes
Learn to fly a drone or a model plane. **Tell** friends what makes them stay in the air.	**Re-write** my favorite book or story as a play. **Make** costumes and add music. **Perform** play	**Create** a scene to **photograph**. **Build** a miniature town or nature scene.	**Sew** by hand or sewing machine. **Recycle** old clothes into something new.
Build a race track - time how fast cars can go & how to increase speed. **Keep records**.	**Set** up **and care for** fish **aquarium**. **Write** or **draw** what I observe each week	**Make BINGO games** to play use math spelling and other things I learn this year – play!	**Read About** whales & dolphins then **draw and write** my own book about them

Examples of How to Translate Interests into Goals
Copyright © 2020 Everfield Press

Collect recipes from different countries and cultures. **Make** special meal experiences for my family.	**Use tools** from the tool chest for a project. **Measure** & **Build** a toy, bench, shelf, or catapult! or anything!	**Research &** **draw** my dream room. **Paint** my room and decorate it or **build a model** of it to decorate.	Help clean a closet. **Sort** clothes or old items - decide what to **recycle**, donate or sell on Craigslist.
Choose music and watch 5 styles of **dancing.** **Learn and practice** 3 styles then **video** myself dancing!	**Read about care of pets** (dogs, birds, lizards, cats, frogs) Help care for pets. Walk or "sit" someone's pet or pets.	**Research musicals** and then select music and Choreograph a dance. **Perform** for my friends or family.	**Learn** rules and **play** outside sports like horseshoes, ring toss, basketball, croquet, running
Learn history & chemistry of soap making. Choose scents, kinds, colors & make for gifts.	**Design** a website I believe in to advertise a service I want to offer	**Tutor** students. Share what I have learned & know how to show.	**Safely Bake** recipes. Measure &, use utensils, and clean up
Organize my research notes in a filing system	**Go bird watching.** Keep a list in a journal.	**Learn to play** guitar. Practice and perform.	**Write** computer code for a game.

Examples of How to Translate Interests into Goals			
Copyright © 2020 Everfield Press			
Read books on Utopias & keep notes in a journal comparing what I felt as I read them. **Write** my own Utopia tale.	**Research** health rules & ads to run a lemonade stand with homemade lemonade with own recipe.	**Make** unique art using photographic paper and sunlight. different shapes objects frame art for gifts.	**Read about** Vegetable gardening – plant, care for and harvest. recipes. **Cook** for family.
Learn about our family car. Help clean the car, check the oil and change a tire. **Keep a record** in my journal of mileage for drives to and from stores.	**Read about** landscaping for my climate. See what plants are available and **sketch** a plan for our yard. Help put this plan into action.	**Study** earth's layers and the origins of volcanoes. **Make** models of 3 types of volcanoes. **Video or draw** it erupt and simulate types of lava.	**Design** and Build a Rube Goldberg contraption to fill a dog bowl with water or to open a door or turn off a light.
Use stencils to create nice posters for a concept or a cause. Vivid images will encourage action!	**Build** my own solar car or machine from a kit. **Show** and tell how it works.	**Practice science** of tricks and illusions. Do a show for my family and then **explain** how it works	**Write or choose a song** to learn to sing. Practice voice techniques and sing!

Examples of How to Translate Interests to Goals

Study	Write	Create a 12	Record
Newton's Laws of motion. Use my toy cars, balls, other objects to show how each law works. Show my family.	letters to the Governor & Congress asking for support for a cause like social justice or endangered species.	month calendar with dates and events printed on it. Use ruler and beautify it with my own photos or art work	day/night temperature, rain fall, humidity, wind speed and cloud cover for 1 day every week in my science journal.
Collect twigs with leaves from trees in my area. Press these and identify them. Mount them in an album or notebook.	**Observe** Insects, Birds & Animals in my yard and **record** their behavior and **identify** them. Keep data in my journal.	**Plan a week of meals** for my family use recipes, make a list shop, record cost then calculate cost per person. Cook meal.	**Read** about world cultures and religions. I will choose at least 3 to compare on a poster or in a written presentation. Share.
Research manicures, pedicures & wash, cut, styling hair.	**Design** & sew my own fashions. Sell Keep data costs/profit	**Create** a surrealistic painting or drawing - explain	**Re-create** famous battles with miniatures using clay.

Integrate Your Child's Interests into Instruction

Nurtured interests may end up being your child's lifelong hobby, or even profession. They will provide your child with meaning and purpose. Some of the items on this list will fit into the category of art, music, or physical education. They are elective subjects that should never be neglected. Art can be used to explore history, science, and math. Music can be used to build memory skills, improve mathematical understandings, and understand history as well. Physical activities have various health benefits, and can even relate to learning math facts, completing science experiments, and even give historical perspectives. The parent can integrate these activities into the curriculum to fuel child involvement as they see fit.

Develop Rules

Rules and structure for achieving the goals you set are especially important. You need to set boundaries and expectations ahead of time while everyone is in a good mood. When children know what is expected of them, they will be less apt to break rules. Make the rules with them. Ask them what the consequences will be if they do not do what is expected. Make sure everyone is happy when you set the rules before there is any confrontation. Here are the basic rules:

1. Listen
2. Respect
3. Take Turns
4. Share
5. Help each other

Be prepared to switch roles between parent, and parent educator. Develop the power structure in your household so you are in control. Outline the rules, identify the workspace, and maintain them. Let your child take ownership of their own work area. Part of the ownership is cleaning up after the work is done. Love your child. *123 Magic* by Thomas Phelan is a discipline system you can use for younger children if you are struggling. The following link to help you establish ground rules https://study.com/academy/popular/homeschool-behavior-contracts-between-parents-children.html is a great reference for creating a parent child contract for homeschooling. Use positive reinforcement. Identify the times they are doing the right thing and praise them. For example, praise your child before they make mistakes. Tell them how wonderful it is that they are sitting and doing their work.

For example, when a child may decide to learn to play the flute, but will not do reading assignments because of flute playing, you must address it. Usually, it is best to save the fun activities for the end of the day. So, a careful plan for fun and most interesting elective activities is essential. However, if you want to incorporate a research paper about the flute in writing time, you might find your child more likely to be enthusiastic about doing that research. Regular times for study and requirements for reading, writing, math, and science are valuable. Do not allow those core subjects to get lost in the mix of elective subjects like art, music, sewing, cooking, building, electronics, or even foreign language. Having a workbook that presents materials taught at grade level in the same spot every day is important. Using *Saxon Math* will keep your child at grade level or beyond grade level.

Assessment

Your child should be involved in their own assessment process. This will build a sense of achievement at the end of the year when it is time to reflect on the year's goal. Going back to that first journal entry from the beginning of the year, will reveal the goals that were set and whether they were achieved. Reflection on each achieved goal will propel them into a future life where setting and meeting goals is second nature. Reading and writing on topics children are interested in builds mastery. Children will naturally discuss their new knowledge with parents. This solidifies further understanding. If they are non-readers, you read what they have written, or have them dictate to you what they want to say every day. Then have them read back what they wrote in their journal daily. Helping your child build a sense of how to set goals and meet them is genuinely a years' worth of growth!

Learning and understanding what interests

your child will be a gift for life. Setting goals, finding goals, developing rules, and assessing oneself leads to success. You will have a jumping-off point for meaningful conversations with your child for years to come.

Chapter 3
Getting Started

Now that you have goals, you can get started. Homeschooling is a 5-step process anyone can do.

1. Write your letter of intent and submit to the school board in the required format.
2. Choose your curriculum and plan.
3. Make and try a schedule weekly, based on what you have planned and tweak it every Monday based on your child's needs.
4. Engage with your child and give them room to explore their interests.
5. Evaluate your child and report the results to the school board either yearly or quarterly based on your state's laws.

Example Letter of Intent

The intent letter can be found online and is different for each school board and jurisdiction. Most of them go something like this.

My son/daughter _____who lives at
_____, will be homeschooled this year
_____. Please know I appreciate the
education provided by _____, but our
family feels this is the safest choice at this time.
Sincerely, _____ (address, phone)

Since a response is not required, be sure that the school board has received a copy of your letter. Many people purchase a Return Receipt request from the post office and keep a copy in their records.

The Curriculum Plan

The curriculum plan should be simple at first. You can add more as you go. If you start with the *Learn at Home Series*, you will have an excellent structure. I also suggest reading the book "*The Well-Trained Mind*" by Susan Wise Baur, which discusses many different resources and curriculum packages, such as Abeka, Calvin, Saxon, Classical Education, etc. *Saxon Math* is highly recommended because it is parent friendly, follows a standards-based scope and sequence and provides step by step explanations, with a plethora of revision problems.

If there is anything that should not fall behind this year, it is math and language arts. The Saxon Math book with parent guide has teacher instructions that are verbatim, especially for second grade. The Buddinwriters program provides a thoughtful structure that introduces higher order thinking skills for writing.

Scheduling

Having lesson plans will keep your day organized. Schedules, notebooks, and journals for you and your child are a must. In addition, an agenda and record-keeping section will keep you organized. Plan the year lightly. Add to the curriculum plan slowly as you learn your child's learning style so you can find materials that best meet their needs. At the very least, the *Learn At Home series, for grades K-6,* will be sufficient. State required textbooks for Grades 7-12 can be purchased online or acquired from the textbook depository. There is a link on the State Department of Education website that shows what textbooks are approved by the state for your child. The *Saxon Math* extends to 12th grade. If finances are limited, places such as your local library give away free books. The Library support group in your town may have all kinds of used home-schooling materials. You can purchase some used textbooks for as little as $2.00. Most school districts will make used textbooks available at their distribution centers. Contact your local schoolboard for more information.

Creating an effective schedule allows for revision. A consistent, structured schedule embraces change and engages learners. For example, you may see your child falling asleep at her desk after lunch and not be able to do math problems. You may want to move your math time to the morning the following week.

Have your structure, give yourself opportunities to change it, and do not give up on it except in exceptional emergencies or sickness. Keep a diary each day, and plan regular time for play, lunch, and breaks.

Engage Your Child

Allow for a dialogue between you and your child. Reflect upon the past week's instruction and together create changes or see if they have ideas based on what they would like to do differently. For instance, say, "How do you feel about how we read the story yesterday? Why did you feel that way?" Or, in regular reading time, let them pick some of the materials they read. Within a consistent structure, build a dialogue with your child so you can maintain a happy homeschool environment.

Evaluation

Evaluating your child's progress is essential and required. Every state has different requirements that can be found online. Most states accept the IOWA test or the

Stanford 9, which can be purchased online and graded through Bob Jones University and various other places. You can also get a portfolio evaluation through a licensed teacher who will go through your child's portfolio and write an evaluation letter. This portfolio should include your child's worksheets, daily journals, and projects completed during the year. Also, some teacher evaluators can do the Brigance Diagnostic up to eighth grade. The standardized test results can help you know if your child can perform at grade level and what exact areas in which they need improvement.

Evaluation day should be a celebration of your child's achievements. Obtain practice tests if they are taking standardized tests and review what they need to know. Prepare your child for the evaluation. Encourage them to reflect upon all their best work and think about what they have learned this year. Tell your child that today is a day you are going to celebrate everything you learned. Some evaluators give certificates and review goals that assess a child's level of success.

Incorporating the Five Steps

Giving room for your child to explore interests starts with the interest inventory. If your child selected BAKE in the interest inventory, then you can buy a cake mix. Let them read the directions and follow them. Discuss the cost and measurement of ingredients as math. You can let them make a taste comparison of different cake flavors. Keep a journal entry of their favorite flavor choices. They can also make a list of foods/recipes they want to cook. Share family recipes with them. Schedule these cooking activities in the afternoon and let them measure, weigh, and add the ingredients. If they selected outdoor games or sports, they could time their activity and set goals for improvement. They can record their own times and keep records of other people doing that sport for comparisons. Each interest can have extensions that help mold your child into a lifelong learner.

After you go through this five-step process over 36 weeks, you will have made a years' worth of growth commensurate with your ability and your child's ability. I believe if you focus on this carefully and mindfully, you may come out of this crazy COVID-19 season with something extra, the title of homeschool mom or dad.

Chapter 4
Interaction

Parental interaction creates a setting where your children are less anxious, more engaged, and have automatic routines that provide a way for them to learn. Anxiety creates an affective filter. The higher the filter, the lower the learning of new information. An anxious child is too busy worrying about protecting themselves from perceived dangers to be able to set aside that worry and focus their attention on reading, writing, science, or arithmetic. When there is a routine that establishes a specific subject for a specific time the child knows what to expect and what they must do. They can become more engaged. A pre-designed morning routine such as "Put the black journal on the table and take out your pink pencil and write five sentences in your journal about what happened yesterday," becomes automatic. They can do this daily. Journal entries will change as a child will explore what they did yesterday. The best thing for children is an environment they can count on. They need to know the routine and that it will not change. Providing a regular routine with joy, excitement, and safety makes a confident child.

Play

Build consistent time in your schedule for play. Parents are creative people who come up with new ways to handle new situations. Children love to play. Children learn important skills through play such as their ability to reason, problem solve, memorize, concentrate, think creatively, and interact with others. For example, encourage your child to learn by matching lids to pots, sorting items such as laundry, silverware, toys, or measuring cups. Additionally, ask them to measure, read the directions while you cook, and keep track of the time. Children do not even realize they learning as they play, but you know they are learning.

Symbolic Play

Most people remember how play made their childhood enjoyable. But we forget how important play is for our children's development. Play is central to young children's learning. You can help children get the most learning from their play. Play helps children to think creatively and solve problems. Language develops through play. Social skills are acquired through play. Play is related to reading and learning to write and building because literacy is very symbolic. For example, when they are using a toy car to represent a real car, they are creating a symbolic relationship. Using a play broom to sweep is learning, also. They are practicing and learning about life skills they will use in the future. Symbolic play is like looking at a word which represents something that is not present. Parents must observe pretend or make-believe, so they can learn about their child's development. This might require some modifications of the play environment.

Importance of Imagination

Make-believe is an important part of cognitive development. Parents should ensure their children engage in make-believe. Do they take on the roles of pretend characters or other people in their lives? Do they use objects in make-believe ways? Do they invent imaginative play situations to play out with their peers? There are a variety of ways that adults can enhance this kind of pretend. One enjoyable way to do this is simply to play along with children and to take a make-believe role. Parents should play with children to make play suggestions, ask questions, and encourage this kind of role playing. Ultimately, the parent should leave the child to play on their own to build independent thinking.

Socialization

Even homeschooled children need the consistency of socialization. Interaction is an important component of learning how to socialize. Tea parties, ball games, board games, birthday parties and other social interactions can be adapted for limiting germ exposure. Follow the CDC guidelines by keeping a safe distance. Outdoor activities are much safer than indoor activities. Have hand sanitizer available and use it vigorously and wash hands with soap and water after every social activity. The child should not rub their nose or eyes until after washing hands. Most of all have a routine for sanitary play.

The more variety you expose your child to the more they will learn. Play outside. Expose them to new environments. Ask your child questions about what they see. See if they can remember what they saw in a place you visit. Check their answers with a picture. Consider interests, provide choices, let them figure things out on their own.

Consistent Parental Interaction

When you observe your child's play you will see social interaction, and verbalization. You can at times interject language as you interact with your child. Encourage language in play settings.

Take a role, try to facilitate more language by asking questions. Try to facilitate some peer interaction if there are friends around. When a child's play is complex and involved, you know they are building thinking skills. If you encourage your child to think about the time, place, immediate circumstances, and action of their imaginings, you will notice their play may be more complex. They will fill in details about what they are playing if you ask them. That is fun. Try asking higher level thinking questions to get your child expressing themselves. You will learn so much about your child. Never stop asking questions. Below is a link to 63 questions if you cannot think about what to ask. Use this link: bit.ly/parentchildquestions .

A child needs space to figure out the answers to questions in play scenarios independently.   Getting involved with play facilitates critical thinking, however the parent should not get too involved. Do not to stay too long or overstay your welcome in a child's playtime. Thinking things through and problem solving are the building blocks of a good education.

Parents need to be very respectful of children's play activities. When parents enhance children's play in these ways and facilitate pretend play, the complexity of a child's play increases. When parents promote social interactions, they are enhancing play, and directly advancing their children's development. Play is a wonderful tool for parents to facilitate building thinking skills for life.

Chapter 5
Materials and Finer Details

A happy, open space to work with no distractions and basic materials for learning is important. The kitchen table is a popular place to set up for homeschooling a child. A dining room table or even a card table set up in the living room will work if you consistently use it, and you and the child are comfortable. A bedroom or playroom is not conducive for learning. Be sure to monitor computer use to avoid distraction, as this is one of the challenges to online learning. Computer availability should be measured for play, research, and study.

LEARNING SPACE CHECKLIST

Cheerful open area with a window view
An area that is not distracting
An area that is not too sunny or hot or cold
Large enough space for parent and child
Chairs the right height for age of child and comfortable
A footstool for young children to reduce strain on short legs
Storage cart or bookcase with drawers for each child's materials.
Good lighting that does not cast shadows on work or hurt the child's eyes.
Table needs a smooth surface, arm room, room for open books and should not wobble. If the surface is pitted or tiled, then use a plastic cutting board or drawing board to provide a smooth firm writing and drawing surface.
Have a trash can handy for the papers, broken pencils, paper towels, from painting, etc.
An electric outlet nearby or an extension cord to accommodate use of electric pencil sharpener or extra lighting.

	A visible clock and a kitchen timer (Ones that twist and ding are suggested.)
	A large clearly visible calendar.

Learning Space Checklist

Now that you have selected a space for learning, you need to gather the learning materials each child will need. Make sure each child keeps an organized and well maintained notebook. They can share art and science materials if necessary, depending upon age differences. You probably already have most of the needed items at home. Each child should have a spill-proof water bottle and a snack pack. Nothing is more devastating than having beautiful artwork or a writing paper covered with water or juice from a knocked over cup. Keep a free-standing paper towel holder with a roll of paper towels on the learning table and a box of tissues. This reduces the number of times a child may need to "get up and get" something interrupting their learning. Each child will also need their own age/level appropriate workbooks, reading books, subject folders, student atlas, a student dictionary, and journals. Each child needs scissors that are comfortable for their hand size (special ones for left-handed if required). A clear plastic shoe bin or food container with a lid or a clean plastic dishpan can be used for holding each child's materials. Below is an example of a learning materials checklist.

	LEARNING MATERIALS CHECKLIST Copyright © 2020 Everfield Press
	2 sharpened pencils with good erasers
	2 blue or black ball point pens
	1 pair scissors
	1 set of 12 or 24 erasable colored pencils
	1 - 12" ruler
	1 - 6" ruler
	1 small pencil sharpener designed to contain Shaved wood from sharpening.
	1 – plastic roll of scotch tape
	2 – glue sticks
	1 – bottle white glue
	4 bookmarks (Reading, Math, Science, Journal)
	1 pack or set of smaller colored post-it-notes
	1 art drawing pad or sketchbook
	1 magnifying glass or magnifying plastic sheet
	1 journal – composition book

Learning Materials Example

There will be a variety of materials needed for science and elective activities, including those special interest goals. Many of these materials will probably be present in your home already.

This chart is an example of items that you can find in your home. They include:

ITEMS YOU MAY WANT TO GATHER TO HAVE ON HAND Copyright © 2020 Everfield Press
Needles and thread
String
Marbles
Building materials and tools
A kitchen scale
Bamboo toothpicks
Mixing bowls
3 x 5 and 4 x 6 index cards
Poster board
White copy paper
Writing paper
Yarn
Ping pong balls
Balloons
Kitchen for science experiments. measuring cups Spoons
Bamboo skewers
Funnels
Cooking ingredients. are Folder for each subject or special project
Colored construction paper
Envelopes and letter stationary

Example of Materials Found in the Home

Do not panic. Items you do not have are not usually expensive and most can be found at your discount store. If there are things you cannot get or cannot afford then skip those activities.

Chapter 6
Resources

There are five important resources you must take into consideration when you homeschool.

1. Rely on your state's Department of Education web site.
2. Find your local homeschool educator groups and webpages. Locate and join their Facebook groups, or lists.
3. Identify book providers such as your library and Amazon.com.
4. Meet other parents who are going through the same things as you.
5. Join Educator groups such as HSLDA (Home School Legal Defense Association) and FPEA (Florida Parent-Educators Association). Everything you need is there for you if you ask for it.

Your State Department's Website

Parents have been guided on how to get started. Some states are different and policies change. Contact your state's Department of Education and local school board for guidance on the process of homeschooling your child. The Department of Education provides practice tests for any subject your child is learning. Many states have all the standards for your child's grade available online to make sure they are working on grade level. Even though you are choosing to homeschool your child, you must still prove that they have made a year's worth of growth commensurate with their ability.

Local Homeschool Educator Groups

Wherever you live, there is most likely a local homeschool group with a Facebook page that will keep you informed. Homeschool groups can help you understand the local resources that are available to you. Homeschool parents like to share. They like to find out what you are doing, and perhaps arrange appropriate safe social distancing gatherings that your child can participate in.

Book Providers

Getting the books, you need for your endeavor is simple. You can order them on Amazon, but the cost can add up. After you have purchased and completed a few workbooks, you may want to depend on the local library for reading material that matches your child's interests. Another option is to purchase used books. Abe's books is an excellent resource for used books: https://www.abebooks.com/books/Textbooks/, Amazon, eBay, Craigslist, and your school board are some of the resources that can help. Start with a list from your child's assigned school and find out what books they would be using in school, so you can try to use the same books. In addition, scholarship options are available for parents who homeschool.

The Learn at Home Series

Let your child know they can count on something regularly. *The Learn at Home Series* found at this link: bit.ly/learnathomebook lends itself to this type of consistency. The series provides a book for each grade with a set of teacher lesson plans for each week. It also provides worksheets to support the plans and experiments. As stated before, the series can be used as a complete curriculum if you do all the extension activities. Since you will tailor a program to your child's needs and abilities, it is a good place to start the weekly lesson plans provided for you in grades 1-6. You can use these plans for states that require documentation. The lesson plans are like regular teacher lesson plans with 180 school days or 36 weeks as required by most states.

Parental Support

Parents need support from other homeschooling parents. Talking to another homeschool parent who has a child the same age as your child can help. Knowing what struggles other parents have and what achievements they have made can encourage you. It is important to compare notes and get advice that will help you be a better homeschool educator. As you learn and grow along the homeschooling journey, you can offer advice that can help others.

You are not alone. Building a homeschool community is possible through all the following support groups. Join the Parent Educator Association and attend their annual homeschool conferences. An added suggestion is to join the Homeschool Legal Defense Association. These organizations provide amazing online resources that can help you develop your strategies for homeschooling. Visit their sites and decide for yourself. Facebook has some sites in your community. Both organizations provide information and defend you in court if your school board wants to take away your right to homeschool. These options will help you find other homeschooling families in your area.

Evaluator Lists

Karen Porter is a Nationally Board-Certified Teacher, Director of Loga Springs Academy, and has been teaching for 36 years. She has been doing homeschool evaluations for over 15 years. She believes homeschooling can work very well for some families. Some of her homeschooled clients have attended Harvard, Alfred University, UF, Santa Fe, and other colleges after their course of home study. She recommends you carefully find an evaluator whom you can rely on yearly. There are many web sites to find a suitable evaluator.

Using the Umbrella School Technique

Once you have started the homeschooling process, you can still get help from well-seasoned teachers. If you are still not comfortable homeschooling on your own, you can use an umbrella school as a guide. An umbrella school is an alternative education path that can serve you by making sure you meet governmental educational requirements. Each umbrella school is different in what they provide and charge. Some have group classes, a structured curriculum, sports, field trips, all types of evaluation, and more.

The Catherine Eileen Academy at CatherinEileenAcademy.org is a reputable umbrella school. They have the sound philosophy of individualized instruction, student centered learning, and developing higher order thinking skills.

The Academy can help you with the following virtual options:

- Academic Curricula
- Electives and Individual Project Learning
- Group or Individual Teaching
- Tutoring
- Academic Counseling & Support
- Evaluations by Florida Certified Teachers
- Official Transcripts & Diplomas
- Full-service Records Department

Personal Perspective

Each family finds their own unique way to homeschool that fits the learning style and temperament of their child. I personally learned a lot from Susan Wise Baur's book because she talks about all the details and does not praise one way to homeschool. Baur presents many curricula and approaches. She lets you choose what you think will work best in her book, *The Well-Trained Mind.* When I joined the North Florida Homeschooler's Association, I gained a lot of insight. When I went to the Florida Parent Educator's Conference, I was presented with a great deal of information that made me a better homeschool

parent.

Chapter 7
Book Lists to Read

Book lists are subjective: they play a helpful role in your curriculum. Google the book list for your child's grade. You can incorporate what students are reading at the most elite schools into your program. Parents need to decide which books are suitable. Below is a link to an article that touches on that subject: bit.ly/booklistforsummerreading

The Critique Process

There are plenty of lists created by others. But you can make your own list by using your child's interest inventory and see if you can find books to match their interests. Award-winning books will maintain a higher interest and percolate your child's love of reading. Feel free to choose from various titles and read parts of some books. Read the whole book when there is motivation. Homeschooling allows you to do this for recreational reading. Here is a review by Diane Stranz of the *Learn at Home Series*. It shows how literature should be embraced. Appreciate what you have in a book. Criticize what you do not like!

Find your own favorite books. Use discernment as Diane has. Do not be afraid to critique what you find.

Diane Stranz

Diane Stranz is a successful homeschool mom. She thinks about how she teaches her children and what curriculum to use. Diane is a shining example of how to use the best part of the resources you have and how to discern what you do not want to use. Read portions of what she has to say about the *Learn at Home* book she purchased for her child below:

"Of course, this [The Learn at Home Book] is not a complete curriculum: but you would be

amazed at how much curriculum help you can get from this 384-page book priced at under $10 (for a used copy)! I cannot TELL you how many times this book, with its level of detail and week-by-week ideas for lesson plans, has helped to calm me down and reassure me that 'it can be done.'

I do agree with reviewers who express the hope that the publisher will update and (for one thing) choose more readily available books for the reading list. I purchased about 3/4 of the books recommended, and they all seem like fine books, but yes it is true that most of them are not ones you will find at your public library -- and that is a drawback if you are on a tight budget like I am.

You can see more of what she has to say at:

https://www.amazon.com/gp/customer-reviews/R155HKYHQJYBKE/ref=cm_cr_dp_d_rvw_t tl?ie=UTF8&ASIN=156189513X

Recommended Books

As a homeschool evaluator and curriculum developer my favorite books are:

- *Writing to Respond: Practice and Assessment: Cultivating Habits of Writing in Grades 3-5 (WRT Workbooks)* by Dr. Martha Joseph Watts.
- *The Story of the World* by Susan Wise Baur, books 1,2,3, and 4.
- *The Well-Trained Mind* by Susan Wise Baur, *Learn at Home Series* by American Education.
- *Saxon Math Complete kits,* by Saxon Publishers.

I also suggest reading Caldecott Award Winning books for the younger grades, and Newberry Award-Winning books for the upper grades. The most recent books are very timely. Susan Wise Baur has a history series called *The Story of the World* that can be used as bedtime reading that will cover world history from the beginning of time to modern days. This four-book series is written in an easy-to-relate-to narrative. Workbooks can be purchased for each book that test reading comprehension as well as historical facts.

Media Extensions

Documentaries about historical topics in books can extend exploration. There are several ways to incorporate technology. Visit historical places of interest virtually. Research facts about a time in history online. Watch documentaries. Play a scavenger-hunt games with the videos you watch. For instance, have a child write down as many things they think will be in the video. Count the correct predictions. This activity can help your child stay focused while they watch the video. Have the child circle their correctly predicted items while watching the video. Reflection stimulates connections to the history. Have your child write what they remembered from their predictions in their journal. Re-reading the journal entry aloud reinforces memory, writing, and reading skills.

Chapter 8
Teaching Language Arts

Be patient if your child is not reading or writing in the prescribed manner. While you help your child master reading and writing, you will see them develop over time. National guidelines and State standards offer basic benchmarks needed to be reached for each grade. But children do not come in standard little packages that perform exactly as the state commands. They tend to have individual personalities that learn and grow at a unique, beautiful lovely pace that shines differently for each child.

Exposure

The child will learn to read and write through exposure, repetition, telling their story to you, and listening to you tell their story to them. Have them read daily for at least half an hour to an hour, that matches their attention span. Parents can read to children, children can read to parents, or children can read on their own (depending on their age). Follow through with discussion of the books. Ask your child higher level thinking questions when you discuss the books. Examples are: What is the motivation of the main character? Why did the characters do what they did? These are questions that require more than a yes or no answer.

The Journal

The writing journal is a crucial tool to use to write and reflect daily. Have patience, compassion, and understanding if your child is not writing. Before your child learns to write, you can write down what they have to say. Take time, breathe, and respect their story. Try not to laugh if you think their ideas are funny. You do not want to embarrass your child. Read the journal to each other from time to time. Have fun with the process. For families, each child can have their personal journal and share their writing and thoughts with their siblings in daily writing time. Older children should be responsible for creating their own rules of journal writing. They should be expected to write a set amount of words in your established contract. Make a special effort to praise your child when they are following through with their expectations.

Structured Writing

In addition to journaling a good homeschooling approach has dedicated structured writing time. Structured writing time includes writing for specific purposes and using defined structures. The *WTR* (*Writing To Respond*) https://www.amazon.com/Writing-Respond-Tests-Martha-Joseph-ebook/dp/B0793P8R81 process will help you craft thoughtful essays. To view language arts benchmarks, see the bulleted list on page 57. You will find the stages of reading and writing in a rough synopsis for each year that shows what your child should be learning.

Second Language Acquisition

The standard curriculum in the United States does not include a second language in the early grades. Evidence proves the excitement of learning a new language is the highest in the early grades. High school requires two years studying a second language in most states. Opening the door to new languages and cultures at an early age will open a new world for your child. When your child returns to public school, they will be prepared for upper grade study.

There are many second language learning programs online such as Duolingo. If your child becomes interested in learning a language, consider writing down what they are learning in a dedicated notebook. Keep a record of the numbers, letters, colors, shapes, etc. to reflect upon at the end of the year. It will help build literacy skills in their own language. Many countries teach second languages in early grades with great success. Learning a new language can make your child more proficient in the mechanics of your native language, as

well. *The Complete Book of Spanish* builds interest in Spanish at home for the early grades.
https://www.amazon.com/Complete-Book-Spanish-Grades/dp/0769685641

General Language Arts Standards

Below are the general standards for each grade level. Consult your State Department of Education for your state's specific grade level standards.

- **Grade K**
  - Recognize all letters and numbers.
  - Write all letters and numbers 1- 20, count to 100.
  - Know all the letter sounds.
  - Read and write the 20 Dolch sight words. *(The Dolch Sight Words list is the most used set of sight words. Dr. Edward William Dolch (1930-40's) developed the list by studying the most frequently occurring words in children's books of that era. The list contains 220 "service words" plus 95 high-frequency nouns).*
    (Sightwords.com, 2020)

- o Understand literacy and how to read a book.
- **Grade 1**
  - o Read and Write sentences.
  - o Know 40 or more sight words.
  - o Begin to write a paragraph.
- **Grade 2**
  - o Read and write sentences.
  - o Learn how to write a paragraph with a topic sentence with three supporting sentences, and an ending sentence.
  - o Read early reader books with short paragraphs.
- **Grade 3**
  - o Read and write sentences.
  - o Learn the mechanics of essays.
  - o Write an essay with an introductory paragraph, three supporting paragraphs, and a concluding paragraph.
  - o Read lower-level chapter books and move to more difficult chapter books.
  - o Develop a grammatical sense.
- **Grade 4**

- o Understand various genres of literature.
- o Have command of narrative and expository writing of the five-paragraph essay.
- o Read chapter books and develop responses to literary questions that involve higher-order thinking.
- o Diagram sentences grammatically.
- **Grade 5**
  - o Recognize various genres of literature.
  - o Develop further command of narrative and expository writing of the five-paragraph essay.
  - o Read chapter books and develop responses to literary questions that involve higher-order thinking.
  - o Build knowledge of the nonfiction genre in writing and reading.
  - o Develop an understanding of the analyzing text.
  - o Develop vocabulary use and parts of speech.
  - o Study syntax and grammar.
- **Grade 6**

- o Explore the complexity of various genres of literature.
- o Have command of narrative and expository writing of the five-paragraph essay.
- o Read chapter books and develop responses to literary questions that involve higher-order thinking.
- o Build knowledge of the nonfiction genre in writing and reading.
- o Analyze text.
- o Exposure to literature with mature themes.
- o Read classical literature.
- o Employ the different genres in writing.
- o Analyze complex text.
- o Develop vocabulary use and parts of speech.
- o Understand synonyms, homonyms, and antonyms.
- o Continue study of syntax and grammar.
- **Grade 7**
  - o Continue reading various genres of literature.

- o Master narrative and expository writing of the five-paragraph essay.
- o Read chapter books and develop responses to literary questions that involve higher-order thinking.
- o Build knowledge of the nonfiction genre in writing and reading.
- o Analyze more complex texts.
- o Continue reading literature with mature themes.
- o Read classical literature.
- o Build vocabulary by exploring suffixes, prefixes and root words.
- o Continue study of synonyms, homonyms, and antonyms.
- o Continue study of syntax and grammar.
- **Grade 8**
    - o Continue exploration of various genres of literature.
    - o Extend practice of narrative and expository writing of the five-paragraph essay.
    - o Read chapter books and develop responses to literary questions that involve higher-order thinking.

- o Extend assessment of the nonfiction genre in writing and reading.
- o Extend analysis of text.
- o Continue reading literature with mature themes.
- o Further investigate classical literature.
- o Extend vocabulary use and parts of speech.
- o Add study of Latin root words, prefixes, and suffixes.
- o Extend synonyms, homonyms, and antonyms.
- o Further study syntax and grammar.
- **Grade 9**
  - o Have command of various genres of literature.
  - o Extend practice of narrative and expository writing of the five-paragraph essay.
  - o Read chapter books and develop responses to literary questions that involve higher-order thinking.
  - o Advance knowledge of the nonfiction genre in writing and reading.

- o Analyze text. Consider metaphors, similes, symbolism, analogies, etc.
- o Consider literature with more mature themes through comparison.
- o Read classical literature.
- o Develop vocabulary use and parts of speech.
- o Understand synonyms, homonyms, and antonyms.
- o Study syntax and grammar.
- o Study a second language to learn basic phonemic awareness and grammar structure.
- **Grade 10**
  - o Integrate literature genres with course of study.
  - o Extend practice of narrative and expository writing of the five-paragraph essay.
  - o Read chapter books and develop responses to literary questions that involve higher-order thinking.
  - o Advance knowledge of the nonfiction genre in writing and reading.

- o Analyze text. Consider metaphors, similes, symbolism, analogies, etc.
- o Consider literature with more mature themes through comparison.
- o Read classical literature.
- o Develop vocabulary use and parts of speech.
- o Understand synonyms, homonyms, and antonyms.
- o Study syntax and grammar.
- o Study a second language to learn basic phonemic awareness and grammar structure.
- **Grade 11**
  - o Integrate literature genres with course of study.
  - o Extend practice of narrative and expository writing of the five-paragraph essay.
  - o Read chapter books and develop responses to literary questions that involve higher-order thinking.
  - o Advance knowledge of the nonfiction genre in writing and reading.

- o Analyze text. Consider metaphors, similes, symbolism, analogies, etc.
- o Consider literature with more mature themes through comparison.
- o Read classical literature.
- o Develop vocabulary use and parts of speech.
- o Understand synonyms, homonyms, and antonyms.
- o Study syntax and grammar.
- o Study a second language to learn basic phonemic awareness and grammar structure.
- **Grade 12**
  - o Integrate literature genres with course of study.
  - o Extend practice of narrative and expository writing of the five-paragraph essay.
  - o Read chapter books and develop responses to literary questions that involve higher-order thinking.
  - o Advance knowledge of the nonfiction genre in writing and reading.

- o Analyze text. Consider metaphors, similes, symbolism, analogies, etc.
- o Consider literature with more mature themes through comparison.
- o Read classical literature.
- o Develop vocabulary use and parts of speech.
- o Understand synonyms, homonyms, and antonyms.
- o Study syntax and grammar.
- o Study a second language to learn basic phonemic awareness and grammar structure.

Once you are aware of the general standards, you can instruct your child accordingly. Exposure to good literature and positive instruction will enhance writing skills. Journal practice will build writing fluency. Structured writing will heighten the quality of their writing techniques. Second language instruction will build grammar and syntax awareness. Each year has different benchmarks. Knowing where your child is performing in this sequence will give you a good starting point for your instruction.

Chapter 9
The Process of Teaching Writing

This book has been written with co-author, Dr. Martha Joseph Watts. She has been an elementary, middle, and high school teacher since 1990. Dr. Watts has been a Professor of Language Arts at The University of the Virgin Islands. She has a deep understanding of teaching of writing to all student groups. During her tenure at the University, she developed talk-writing strategies to help English language learners become confident writers. Her experience with learners in diverse settings influenced her publications on the *Writing to Respond Process* (WTR). This technique is widely used to teach writing in grades K-12 worldwide. Below, Dr. Watts presents a brief explanation of the process.

Writing and the Home Schooler

As home schooling parents, you have the best opportunity to develop confident writers. This is only possible after you have learned to debunk what you have learned about teaching writing. Let us explore the myths that stop you from being the best writing instructor you can be.

Myth I: Writing is hard

The hardest part of the writing process may be the inability to communicate. For example, a mute or severely mentally disabled child may have a more difficult time learning to write. All children can become more confident writers. All children can have a meaningful experience expressing their thoughts and ideas.

What is the pre-requisite for writing? It is the ability to communicate orally by first understanding and then responding. If your child can listen, understand, and respond to questions orally, your child can already write. This is true because writing is thinking before print.

Another prerequisite to writing is having the ability to communicate your thoughts and ideas orally. All children should be encouraged to talk. The habit of talking and responding in complete sentences leads to a child who can thoughtfully communicate ideas on paper. At this time, you can begin to work in a written format.

Myth 2: Writing starts at a specific grade level

A common myth is that most structured writing begins at grade two or three. But children are able (and do) develop writing skills as soon as they can listen to and understand language. When children begin to draw pictures to express what they are thinking they are writing.

Some second and third grade children have dysgraphia, and other processing problems. Physically, some children cannot put their words on the page. They still have a capacity to think, share, and discuss. However, they may not be writing their thoughts on paper as soon as their peers. Accommodate non-writers by continuing to support their artistic expression or letting them dictate their thoughts while you write them down. Then children can copy what you have written. For children with processing issues, consider meaningful writing practice such as the *Abeka Cursive Writing Skillbook* that can be found at the following link at bit.ly/handwritingbook

Children who need to improve their physical writing ability will also be able to learn dictionary skills. For children with processing problems, the graphics in this skill book make meaningful connections to words.

Expelling the Myths

Educators must dispel myths one and two. The next steps in the outline below will put the parent educator in the best position to develop their children's writing. As previously discussed by Karen Porter, the Writing to Respond Process (WTR) build's mastery as parents move through the benchmarks. The steps below will guide the parent through the process. These techniques apply to emerging writers and readers as well as advanced readers and writers.

One: Engage your child in the constructive habit of sophisticated conversation

Let us examine this scenario: Your child is in the car or shopping center with you. Instead of gaming on the phone, engage in conversations around things you observe. For example, naming produce or comparing produce. How can you tell a cantaloupe from a watermelon? What is different about people's interactions with each other in the supermarket? How do you feel about self-checkout instead of a cashier's assistance? Ask questions based on your child's educational level. The idea is to get children in the habit of thinking of questions and responding to them in complete sentences.

Two: Connect writing to reading, or some other form of text such as audio, media, art, or cartoon.

Having interests to connect to will elevate the child's willingness to go through the process. Once you have identified the book, movie, artwork, cartoon, or event that connects with your child's interest to the writing, get ready to read, listen or observe. If the child is reading, ensure that the text is on their performance level, not below or above because the focus is on writing, not reading. For younger children, the adult will do the reading. Pay attention to the steps for asking questions *before*, *during* and *after* reading activities.

Steps for Asking Questions

Before Reading:

Identify the title, author, and illustrator. Talk about the title. Make predictions. Discuss any new word from the title that may clarify meaning.

During Reading:

Read, pause, ask clarifying, and predicting questions. To ensure understanding, ask "right there" or recall questions. Ask questions about the characters, plot, and other elements of the story. Once you have reached the end, ask for a summary. Please model summarizing. To summarize is to write the short version. Bloom's Taxonomy gives a visual representation of how children learn the thinking/reading/writing connection. Below are the questions you should ask while you read.

Bloom's Taxonomy Question Stems To Be Used **During Reading**. Questions on the bottom of the pyramid. Copyright © 2020 Buddin Writers

Knowledge	
What happened after ...?	How many ...?

Who was it that . . .?	Can you name the—in the story . . .?
Described what happened at . . .?	Who spoke to . . .?
Can you tell why . . .?	Find the meaning of . . .?
What is. . . .?	Which is true or false?
Comprehension	
Can you write a brief outline of ...?	What do you think might happen next?
Who do you think of . . .?	What was the main idea of . . .?
Who was the key character in . . .?	Can you write in your own words for . . .?
Application	
Do you know another instance where . . .?	Could this have happened in . . .?
Can you group by characteristics such as . . .?	What factors would you change if . . .?

Bloom's Taxonomy Questions During Reading

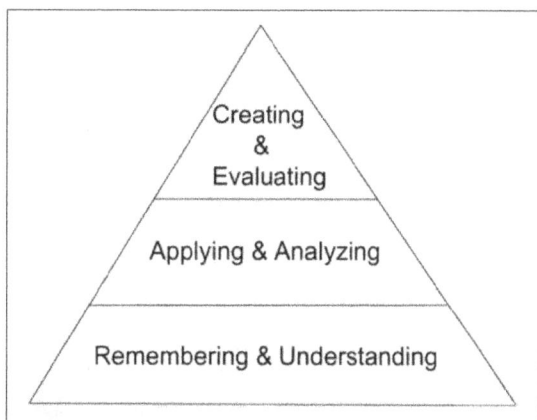

Blooms Taxonomy

The concept of Blooms Taxonomy above is that learners build knowledge progressively. The higher order thinking skills are at the top and the lower order thinking skills at the bottom provide a scaffolding for readers to conduct higher thinking. See examples Blooms Taxonomy Higher Order thinking questions you will use after reading below.

After Reading:

During reading, the child paid attention to all the lower order thinking questions that provided a scaffolding for higher questions to be answered. Now questions will stir thinking for writing. These are higher order thinking questions. Use the higher order questions below after you read.

BLOOMS TAXONOMY QUESTIONS AFTER READING Leading to written responses. Copyright © 2020 Buddin Writers

Analysis	
Which events could have	What happened . . .?
Why did . . . changes occur?	How was this similar to . . .?
What was the underlying theme of . . .?	What do you see as other possible outcomes?
If . . . happened, what might the ending have been?	Can you compare your . . . with that presented in . . .?
Synthesis	
What are some of the problems of . . .?	Can you create new and unusual uses for . . .?
Can you design a . . . to . . .?	Why not write a song about .?
Can you see a possible solution to . . .?	Can you develop a proposal which would . . .?
Can you write a new recipe for a tasty dish?	If you had access to all resources how would you deal with .?
Evaluation	
Can you defend your position about . . .?	How would you have handled . . .?
Is there a better solution to ..?	Judge the value of . . .?
What do you think about . . .?	How effective are .?
What changes to . . . would you recommend?	Do you think . . . is a good or a bad thing?

Examples of this process in action are in Appendix A. This worksheet helps the instructor guide the student to ask questions while they read and write. In the WTR process we call it the *React, Question,* and *Suggestion* phase which is included in the worksheets in the Appendix A, B, and C.

Reaction Phase

No matter the age of the child, the parent asks questions that connect with the child's feelings. Ask the child if there is something from the story that makes them happy, sad, surprised, upset etc.? Be sure to ask about just one feeling. Then ask the child to identify the part or event in the story or piece that caused the feeling. Your child would be practicing evidence-based thinking.

For the *Grades K-2* child, this process is done orally. If parents record the exchange it will be easy for them to write the child's responses. These responses can utilize for future reading materials. You can also allow your child the opportunity to draw that response. Remember the most important aspect of this process in the "thinking". The idea that your child can respond with text-evidence is preparing your child for informative writing. Below is a YouTube link that provides an example of writing instruction.

https://www.youtube.com/watch?v=2rhkdcGUULl

For the *Grades 3-5* child, move from oral to written. The child responds orally but writes a sentence that expresses the feeling and evidence to support. For example, a child might say: *I feel disappointed about the story because the parent sent the little girl into the forest all by herself.* If your child is a struggling writer, you can write the sentence and they can copy the question. Other examples can be found in the workbook *Writing to Respond Practice and Assessment 3-5* also available on Amazon: https://buddinwriters.com/products/ols/products/writing-to-respond-practice-and-assessment-3-5 Appendix A is a sample of response worksheet.

The reaction phase is also where you ask questions that evoke comparison, cause and effect, or argumentative responses. This means that the WTR process can be used with daily instruction. Although it does not always have to result in writing, frequent use of the process helps you solidify the thinking process needed for writing with confidence.

Question Phase

Often when we think of a question in a process, the question comes from the educator. During this moment in the WTR process, give students the opportunity to ask clarifying questions of the author themselves. For example, after reading a short article on dolphins, one child asked, "Why do dolphins swim in groups? The article had included that detail without adding any reasons. This question opens the opportunity for discussion and research. Do not underestimate this opportunity to expand thinking beyond the text.

Suggestion Phase

At this stage, your child is responding to the reading on the highest level of Bloom's Taxonomy. This is the creative space. Provide opportunities for solving problems. Collect evidence from multiple sources. Actively produce responses, including personal experience. Ask the right questions and you will see your child thinking and responding on a higher level. Be prepared to do a lot of probing. A child is most likely to avoid this section by stating, "I do not have any suggestion." Therefore, to combat that possibility present your own synthesis questions. Here is an example: *"What should Little Red Riding Hood's parents have done differently?"* Asking such questions will encourage your child to think deeply and write profoundly. The following self-check list helps your child evaluate this thinking process.

SELF-EVALUATION FOR SUGGESTION PHASE Copyright © 2020 Buddin Writers	
Self-Check: Ask yourself: Did I ...	Yes, or not yet
...identify and name the author and title of the article or story?	
...summarize or use two sentences to tell only the important information about the story?	
...write my reactions to what I heard?make connections to my life or to situations I know about?	
...ask questions to clarify my curiosity?	

Evaluation for the Suggestion Phase

The goal of WTR is to develop confident writers. Thus, WTR is a lifelong process. Once your child has had a response under each section of the graphic organizer, it is time to practice sentence combining. Your child will combine all five sentences to form one paragraph. You can see an example in Appendix B of how a student would complete the worksheet, and an example of what that model would look like if it were followed in student writing time in Appendix C.

Assessment

Assessment is a valuable tool to help your child improve their writing. It is part of the reflection and editing process. When your child revisits a piece of work as many times and evaluates it before sharing it with you, they take pride in their work. You can use the check list on the preceding page.

Grading

Grades 3-5

If you choose to grade your child, you will need a rubric that measures effort, quality work, and skill improvement. Good writers write often. Confidence will be built by regular writing that is edited and improved upon. The homeschool evaluator will be the best judge of your child's improvement in writing. A good portfolio will provide writing samples that show how your child moved through the editing process. Mastery of each academic writing skill will be achieved through continual practice. You can provide a non-threatening environment.

Grades 6-12

The process is similar to that of the grade 3-5, except that during the reaction phase we strongly recommend focusing on the type of question that will support the form of essay writing that you are focusing on at that moment. For example, if you are focusing on cause and effect essay writing, then ask analysis questions that will elicit cause and effect responses. For example, after reading an article on Bird Racing, students were asked, "What effects might continual animal racing have on animals? For the time you are focusing on cause and effect ask the questions that promote that thinking. You can transfer that process to ordinary conversations around the house. Once your child has developed that level of analytical thinking, your child is now ready to write in response to narrative, informative, argumentative, and rhetorical writing prompts.

See Writing to Respond Practice and Assessment 6-12 for more examples and suggestions in Appendices A, B, and C.

Packets are available for each of the essay writing formats such as narrative, informative, argumentative, and rhetorical at www.buddinwriters.com/product/packets Each packet has seven suggested lessons that include step-by-step guide, rubrics and Bloom's Question Stems, graphic organizers and worksheets.

In conclusion, Dr. Watts' experience had led her to master several Language Arts teaching techniques. She imparts her wisdom to help other parents offer quality instruction to their children. The most important advice she can offer is engaging children as early as possible by asking them questions that provoke higher level thinking. Engaging children in conversation is a key component to reading and writing. Dr. Watts passionately believes that all children are learners but Dr. Watts cautions parents about comparing different levels of success.

Chapter 10
Teaching Science and History

Science

The state-mandated curriculum for science is usually broken down into various scientific experiments. The early grades include several hands-on experiential activities emphasizing scientific thinking. They introduce all the sciences. The upper grades call for Life Science in Grade 7, Earth Science in Grade 8, Physics, Biology, and Chemistry.

The Scientific Method

The basic scientific method is used to explore all the sciences taught. It is a set of questions to solve problems. The *scientific method* has six steps.

1.Observe (ask what is happening here?)
2.Question (ask why this is happening?)
3.Hypothesize, (ask if……then what?)
4. Predict results (forecast possibilities.)
5. Build a process to test it (ask how?)
6. Explain your findings (hypothesize or predict more. This last step responds to all the other previous five steps.)

The scientific method of questioning devised by Sir Francis Bacon (https://www.khanacademy.org/science/high-school-biology/hs-biology-foundations/hs-biology-and-the-scientific-method/a/the-science-of-biology) is used in all scientific endeavors including chemistry, physics, geology, and psychology. Parents and children can ask different questions to perform different tests depending on areas of study. However, you will use the same core approach to find answers to your questions that are logical and supported by evidence you uncover.

The Sequence of Science Instruction

Schools vary on the sequence of the sciences they teach. For instance, Marion County, Florida, teaches Earth Science in the 6th, Life Science in the 7th, and Physical Science in the 8th grades. The math for physical science makes it best taught at the end of middle school. For example, the Laws of Motion are algebraic formulas learned in upper middle school grades. The spiral approach is another option to sequencing your science curriculum. The spiral approach in which pieces of each branch of Science are covered each year is what Alachua County Florida employs.

The sequence of high school science is more specific. High school usually has Biology in 9th, Chemistry in 10th, Physics in Grade 11th, and Biology 2 in 12th grades. Some states include additional sciences such as Anatomy & Physiology, Environmental Science, Physics 2, Forensic Science, Astronomy, and Wildlife Science.

For each lower grade, the *Learn at Home Series* or books like *180 Days of Science* provide hands-on activities. These currently popular activities cover the scope and sequence of the grade-level science. The later grades require textbooks that focus on each branch of science. Refer to the depository already discussed for books for the sciences taught in the older grades.

Citizen Science

If you want a challenge and would like to support actual scientists who are struggling to preserve and protect wildlife, you can reach out to nature preserves. These special resources are losing funding. Some of them do outreach to schools to sustain their conservation efforts. They are losing funding because of Covid-19. Ask them to teach your child about their preservation work through Zoom. For example, contact Chase Pirtle for online experiential science interaction with live reptiles at Ashton Biological Preserve at c-biodiversity@hotmail.com. The Preserve can provide instructions on putting together science kits for your child or can even offer science kits (reasonably priced) for some experiments. When schedules permit, for a fee, Ashton Biological Preserve (run by Ashton Biodiversity Research & Preservation Institute, Inc., a non-profit) can arrange a presentation or hands-on science activities in chemistry, physics, ecology, or biology.

The activities include live animals either through Zoom or in-person with lots of Covid-19 safety precautions.

Science Fairs

Local homeschool groups and local schools or organizations can participate in virtual science fairs. Below are two virtual fairs offered in the 2020-2021 school year. In addition, local labs and scientific societies offer mentoring. State and local parks and preserves can help you build additional hands-on activities.

https://ashtonbiodiversity.com/
https://fl02219191.schoolwires.net/Page/504

You may also want to consider helpful district guidance for the middle school curriculum calendar such as https://www.sbac.edu/Page/9169. Alachua County's spiral curriculum integrates all branches of science each year. Use textbooks that match your Schoolboard's science curriculum.

History

When you homeschool, you can sequentially

teach history from the beginning of time until the present day. Most state curricula use a spiral technique usually covering the past two to three hundred years of North American history every year with a different focus on local and national events. From time to time districts touch upon multicultural historic events. When history is taught as a story that covers the entire world, a broader perspective of the world can be reached. *The Story of the World* by Susan Wise Bauer is an excellent resource. Her books are beautifully written and provide a sequential narrative version of history.

Using Timelines

A timeline of events that sequentially progresses through history gives a child a better understanding of time. Each of the books in *The Story of the World* series has a timeline that teaches Early Ancient times, Medieval times, Colonial times, and Modern history. They move from era to era telling specific stories with a broad multicultural representation of each time period. The companion workbooks ask essential questions that are relevant and written in child friendly language. Essential questions promote a grasp of the context of each era. After each story students and parents can dig deeply into the content to continue further exploration. Stories spark conversations so discussion and debate can follow the readings. Many possible extensions in art, music, and media are available online that the whole family can enjoy. For example, if you are reading about Egypt, you can watch a documentary about pyramids as a family.

Why History Matters

Knowledge of history helps parents and students think creatively so they can seek new possibilities. Once they understand the perspective of other times and cultures, they can revisit their own times to make sense of current events. Approaching history in this open-ended manner leads to intelligent comparisons and nurtures higher order thinking. A good history text should ask *why* things happened, to *what* extent they happened, and *how* they happened. Continue to ask higher order thinking questions. This will give children a world view that will open endless possibilities in their lives.

Chapter 11
Teaching Math

Teaching math is a process of asking questions. Making the questions accessible and relevant to your child's life will stimulate a child's interest in math. Skills such as counting money, measuring ingredients, being the banker in a Monopoly game are all part of relevant math instruction. Using good textbooks will also keep interests alive. The basic benchmarks students need to master by grade level in math are:

- **Kindergarten**
    - Introduce number skills writing and recognition.
    - Understand more than, greater than

- o Work with the concept of minus and plus.
- o Solve word problems accordingly.
- **First Grade**
  - o Solve basic one column addition and subtraction.
  - o Solve word problems accordingly.
- **Second Grade**
  - o Solve basic two and three column addition and subtraction.
  - o Begin to borrow and carry.
  - o Learn how to count by 2, 3, 4, and 5.
  - o Begin multiplication Word problems accordingly.
- **Third Grade**
  - o Master multiplication tables.
  - o Continue 2, 3, and 4 column addition and subtraction.
  - o Practice multiplication.
  - o Solve word problems accordingly.
  - o Introduce fractions.
  - o Continue to work on less than and more than, addition and subtraction.
- **Fourth Grade**

- o Continue mastering multiplication.
- o Solve percentage problems.
- o Solve division problems.
- o Practice long division.
- o Continue all other skills.
- o Solve word problems accordingly.
- **Fifth Grade**
  - o Work on percentages.
  - o Begin basic algebraic thinking.
  - o Continue solving three and four column addition, subtraction, multiplication problems.
  - o Start dividing fractions.
- **Sixth Grade**
  - o Solve mixed fractions.
  - o Solve complicated word problems.
  - o Solve pre-algebraic questions.
  - o Work with percentages, and exponents.
- **Seventh Grade**
  - o Solve pre-algebraic questions.
  - o Employ geometric thinking.
  - o Practice graphing.
  - o Solve word problems.
- **Eighth Grade**

- o Solve Pre-Algebraic and Algebraic questions.
  - o Solve fractions problems.
  - o Work with exponents.
  - o Learn about Trigonometric expression.
- **Ninth Grade**
  - o Complete the course of study for Algebra 1.
- **Tenth Grade**
  - o Complete the course of study for Geometry.
- **Eleventh Grade**
  - o Complete the course of study for Algebra 2.
- **Twelfth Grade**
  - o Complete the course of study for Calculus.
  - o Or, complete the course of study for Trigonometry.

Presenting the Scope and Sequence of Knowledge

This list gives a general sense of the

sequence. It is the parent's job to present the scope of knowledge. Saxon has the best program that derives problems in a well thought out way. In the early grades. Saxon teacher textbooks have narratives in each lesson for parents to read to the child. These narratives walk the child through the steps and questions needed for an in-depth understanding. There are other programs such as Math U See, and Abeka Math. Saxon has the best reviews. Their materials are inexpensive.

Learning mathematics is a sequential process. The knowledge base your child learns as they progress through the sequence of instruction scaffolds the next line of instruction. Mastery of each step of the sequence is not necessary to progress to the next step in the sequence. For example, if your child has not mastered their multiplication tables, it does not mean they should not progress to the next step of learning division. Nevertheless, they still need to master their multiplication facts. You can continue to revise and strengthen areas that are not yet mastered while learning new mathematical skills. The parent must be mindful of what their child knows and review areas they are not proficient in as they progress through the curriculum.

Chapter 12
Evaluation and Conclusion

Evaluation

Every state in the USA has varying requirements for homeschooling evaluation. You can find your state's requirements at https://hslda.org/legal. The Commissioner of Education requires local school districts to provide a form for the parent to complete. Some states want an instruction plan, in which case you can use the *Learn at Home book*, *Saxon Math*, or even just list the textbooks already used by your state.   This form usually asks for the child's name, age, address, the guardian's names, and a statement that shows you have homeschooled this year.

The Evaluation Process

Choose the best evaluation process for your child. Make this time a time to celebrate and prepare. Traditionally a test is given over the space of two or three days, or an evaluator performs a one-hour portfolio evaluation. A child who has a learning disability or does not do well with standardized tests, usually performs well on portfolio evaluations. A portfolio evaluation includes samples of your child's outstanding work throughout the school year. This may include completed workbooks, drawings, art projects, their journal, and independent projects. Many children look forward to portfolio evaluations when they reflect on their work and review how they have met the goals they set for the year.

Testing

Testing has one purpose for the state, which is to evaluate that your child has made a "year's' worth of growth commensurate with their ability." That is all your evaluator needs to state in the letter to the school board in Florida. It may be different in other states, so you must carefully read the information on the HSLDA (Home School Legal Defense Association) website at this link https://hslda.org/legal

Preferably you want your child to perform in the ninety-ninth percentile. You can and should look at the evaluation results as a marker to measure what areas your child is weak in and where your child excels. Then you can have data to give your child's teacher in the fall. You can also use testing data to drive your instruction for the following year. If you know what areas are weak and strong you can plan your next year of study accordingly.

Send your results to your local school board. Once you fill out your form, keep a copy of it. Some states require an "In home Instruction Plan" (IHIP). Each district has a form for that too. It is very straightforward.

To comply with your state requirements, a lesson plan section like the one in the Learn at Home series will do. Just be sure you have 180 days of instruction listed with 36 weeks of school and a list of what you are going to do for each day.

A few states require quarterly reports that can be provided from your *Learn at Home* book too.

Standardized tests can be purchased online from Bob Jones University and then mailed in for scoring. Several standardized tests are allowed, such as The Iowa Test of Basic Skills, The California Achievement Test, The Stanford Achievement Test, The Comprehensive Test of Basic Skills, The Metropolitan Achievement Test, The State Education Department Test, and the Stanford 9. They break down the different skills very carefully and report a wider band of skill sets your child has achieved. I suggest this highly for people who are planning to return to public school once it is safe. Teachers will get a paper view of data they can use to plan and prepare their classes for the following year.

If you are planning to homeschool for a while, I suggest you find a homeschool evaluator you will enjoy meeting year after year. Having the same evaluator is rewarding for you, your child, and the evaluator. They will provide a written narrative evaluation that carries weight because they are a certified teacher. They will also gain insight into your child's learning style and have insight a standardized test cannot have.

Appendices D, E, F, and G are samples of a homeschool evaluations. Please note that the first half of the narrative section is for your records and does not necessarily need to go to the schoolboard. Each state requires different items. The State of Florida only requires a 'years of growth' letter that states your child achieved a year's worth of growth. Since a response is not required, be sure that the school board has received a copy of your evaluation. Many people purchase a Return Receipt request from the post office and keep a copy in their records.

Evaluation is a time to Celebrate

After evaluation is over, it is time to celebrate and have a special meal or trip to the park for a day of celebration.

Conclusion

In conclusion, you CAN be a successful homeschool provider! There are several points to take away from this book.

- You are not alone! Find local and national support groups
- Follow instructional guidelines set by your state.
- After you have met those guidelines, tailor instruction to the specific needs and tastes of your child.
- Schooling consistency is a MUST! Make sure your child knows when they are "at school" and when they have down time at home.
- Meet the core (basic) requirements of a well-rounded education. Set goals within the subjects of Language arts (reading and writing), math, and science.
- Your child must meet state standards with yearly testing/evaluation.

The rationale for homeschooling is personal and will unfold as the parent pursues their child's learning path. If the child's needs, interests, and goals drive instruction, then you will have an involved child. When the stage is set (with time for play, discussion, and activities) for a child's success, a unique dance between parent and child begins. This book will enhance the process of asking questions to stimulate curiosity. Whether or not you embrace a full homeschooling schedule, use this book to interact with your child in ways that will facilitate an enquiring mind. The materials, resources, and books you choose will support your journey. In summary, teaching is merely a process of asking questions and discovering answers with your learner.

K .W. Porter and M. J. Watts

APPENDIX A

Identify: Name the title, the author and publication.

_____

_____

Summarize: Use two to three sentences to summarize the article.

_____

_____

_____

Evaluate: React to what you read.

_____

_____

_____

Question: What questions do you have?

_____

_____

Synthesis: What suggestions do you have?

_____

_____

A new word from your reading: _____

6

APPENDIX B
Student's Example of Completed Worksheet

Identify: Name the title, the author and publication.

The article "Orangutan Escapes from Zoo Exhibit" is written by Tyler Shepard and published by clikOrlando.com

Summarize: Use two to three sentences to summarize the article.

A 7-year-old Orangutan escaped its exhibit from a Kansas City zoo on Sunday July 3, 2016. This incident occurred a few days after an 18-year old Orangutan escaped from an exhibit at Busch Gardens in Tampa (Shepard).

Evaluate: React to what you read.

It is amazing that two Orangutans escaped their exhibits around the same time. Maybe Orangutans do not like being held captive.

Question: What questions do you have? Are Orangutans harmful to humans?

Synthesis: What suggestions do you have?

Zookeepers should be more careful about securing the exhibits that house animals with great climbing skills. Or maybe animals like Orangutans should not be captured. They should be left in the wild where they can climb as high as they wish.

A new word from reading:_____ exhibits.

APPENDIX C
Putting it all Together
Now put all responses together in paragraph form.

A Real Home for Orangutans

The article "Orangutan Escapes from Zoo Exhibit" is written by Tyler Shepard. It is published by ClickOrlando.com. The author states that a 7-year-old Orangutan escaped its exhibit from a Kansas City zoo on Sunday July 3, 2016. This incident occurred a few days after an 18-year-old Orangutan escaped from an exhibit at Busch Gardens in Tampa, Florida (Shepard). It is amazing that two Orangutans escaped their exhibits around the same time. Could it be that Orangutans do not like to be held in captivity? I wonder if they are harmful to humans.

I suggest that Zookeepers be more careful about securing the exhibits that house animals with great climbing skills. Or maybe animals like Orangutans should not be captured. They should be left in the wild where they can climb as high as they wish.

Work Cited

Shepard, T. "Orangutan Escapes from Zoo Exhibit". ClickOrlando.com 4 July 2016.

Additional workbook exercises can be purchased at bit.ly/Writingworkbooks

Example of Home School Evaluation Letter for Grades K-11

Johnny Homeschool is the son of Mom Homeschool and Dad Homeschooler who reside at Learning Circle, Anytown, Fl 77777. His birthday is January 23, 2009 and he is 11 years old and in fifth grade. In accordance with the Anytown County and State of Florida policies concerning homeschooling, I, Mrs. Homeschool Evaluator, completed a portfolio review, on July 18, 2020. He is making excellent progress in all areas observed. He is an avid reader and is constantly finding new books that he enjoys reading. He has read Star Wars and Legos Idea books. His portfolio is well organized and reveals the progress he has made.

When the Homeschool family began homeschooling, their goal was to provide a well-rounded advanced educational program with a spirit-led foundation. In addition to achieving these goals, the homeschool family also realized the importance of Johnny's individual learning style. Intertwined within Johnny's academics were opportunities to problem solve.

Johnny has enjoyed this school year. He has an impressive art portfolio that he is proud of. It shows skill and concentration. Johnny loves to read and has mastered reading skills above his grade level. He reads aloud on a lower ninth grade level. He has learned how to read very well this year. He spent the time needed to build mastery of reading and writing with initiative, joyfulness, and diligence. As a result of this focus on academics, he has developed an understanding of the curriculum that exceeds most children in his grade. He is an extremely hard worker. He is very self-motivated and sets a good example. He especially likes to make home movies and do art. These attributes will help him achieve success in the years to come.

Johnny's reading skills are excellent. His fluency is high according to the Brigance Diagnostic Inventory. When given a Fry –referenced story with a ninth-grade textbook-criterion vocabulary of seventy-six words, Johnny was able to read the story aloud. He had difficulty with no more than two words. His comprehension for reading is at a ninth-grade level or beyond. He can sound out words and read fluently at an extremely high level, yet he comprehends at a moderately high level. According to the Brigance Diagnostic Inventory, Johnny can solve single-digit and double-digit addition and subtraction problems, multiplication, adding and subtracting mixed fractions, division, and adding numbers with decimals. His strength is word problems.

Johnny's language skills are also highly developed. He is very verbal and has a highly developed vocabulary. He is using an eclectic system of various texts and readings that match his interest level. Johnny takes online classes for social studies and public speaking.

All of Johnny's accomplishments show that he is ready to be promoted to sixth grade.

APPENDIX E
An Example of a Year's Worth of Growth Letter

July 18, 2020

Dear School Board of Anytown County,

It is with great pleasure I recommend Johnny Homeschool be promoted to sixth grade. He has shown demonstration of educational progress at a level commensurate with his ability. After thorough evaluation I am confident that he is reading and solving math problems above grade level expectations. He also knows reading, social studies, writing, math and science concepts needed for sixth grade and beyond.

Sincerely,

Sincerely,
Mrs. Homeschool Evaluator M.Ed.
Professional Educator
Certificate # 123456
Compassion Place,
Anytown, Florida 77777
evaluator@gmail.com
352-955-2392

APPENDIX F
Example of Home School Evaluation Letter for Graduation

Suzie Homeschooler is the daughter of Mrs. Homeschooler and Mr. Homeschooler who reside at the Great Outdoors Drive, Anytown, FL 77777. Her birthday is October 19, 2002 and she is 18 years old. In accordance with the Alachua County and State of Florida policies concerning homeschooling, I, Mrs. Evaluator, completed a portfolio review, on June 11, 2020. Suzie is making excellent progress in all areas observed. She is an avid reader and is constantly finding new books that she enjoys reading. She has read fifty books this year with an emphasis on building knowledge where her own interests lie. She has read and reported on The Canterbury Tales by Chaucer among other books. Her portfolio is well organized and reveals the progress she has made.

When the Homeschooler family began homeschooling, their goal was to provide a well-rounded advanced educational program with a spirit-led foundation. In addition to achieving these goals, they also realized the importance of Suzie's individual learning style. Intertwined within Suzie's academics were opportunities to problem solve. Suzie was able to master all the twelfth-grade benchmarks in the Sunshine State Standards this year. She spent the time needed to build mastery with initiative, joyfulness, and diligence.

As a result of this focus on the benchmarks, Suzie has developed an understanding of the curriculum that exceeds most children in her grade. She loves math challenges and has developed a special interest in ecology, and wildlife conservation. She has been reading Shakespeare this year and plans to see a performance of a play in town. She is an extremely hard worker. She is very self-motivated and sets a good example. These attributes will help her achieve success in the years to come.

She is excited about graduating and moving on to college work this year. Suzie's language, science, physical education, and math skills are also highly developed for future college work. She has a vision for her future studies and is highly motivated. Her writing demonstrates her abilities that will support her in her future college work. The *Learning Language Arts Through Literature* series has given her a broad and deep understanding of literature. Her science projects and labs have given her a practical sense of science that she will use going forward. She has completed *Saxon Math* and has a firm sense of deriving problems that she will benefit from as she progresses in college. She is physically fit and ran in a half marathon run this year and won first place!

Suzie's portfolio contains proof of mastery. Study of history, science, math, art, reading, language arts and social studies in great depth is evident. Her portfolio schedule shows she reads daily and completes all her school assignments perfectly. Each lesson shows she does not move on to a new problem until she gets the correct answer. She has a love of learning. A special joy shines through when she discusses her academic plans. For all these reasons I recommend that she be conferred for graduation this year.

APPENDIX G
An Example of a Year's Worth of Growth Letter for Graduation

June 11, 2020

Dear School Board of Anytown County,

It is with great pleasure I recommend Suzie Homeschooler graduate from high school this year. She has shown demonstration of educational progress at a level commensurate with her ability. After thorough evaluation I am confident that she is reading and solving math problems above grade level expectations. She also knows reading, social studies, writing, math and science concepts needed for graduation.

Sincerely,
Mrs. Homeschool Evaluator M.Ed.
Professional Educator
Certificate # 123456
Compassion Place,
Anytown, Florida 77777
evaluator@gmail.com
352-955-2392

Reference

Ashton Biological Tortoise Preserve (2020) c-biodiversiy@hotmail.com.

Bauer, S. W., & Wise, J. (2016). *The Well-Trained Mind: A Guide to Classical Education at Home (Fourth Edition)* (Fourth ed.). W. W. Norton & Company.

Bloom, B. S. (1956). *Taxonomy of Educational Objectives, Handbook 1: Cognitive Domain* (2nd edition Edition). Addison-Wesley Longman Ltd.

J'Nai Davis Launches Aunty Marcella Summer Reading Challenge. (2020, July 6). [Video]. YouTube. https://www.YouTube.com/buddinwritersDrWatts

J'Nai Writing In Response to her Reading (WTR):

Step Two Aunty Marcella Summer Reading

Challenge. (2020, July 6). [Video]. YouTube.

https://www.YouTube.com/buddinwritersD

rWatts

Joseph Watts, M. (2020, March 3). *Writing Packets.*

Buddinwriters Academy LLC.

https://buddinwriters.com/product/packets

Porter, K.W. (2020). *Homeschooling.* Everfield

Press. https://www.everfieldpress.com

Porter, K. W. (2018). *Loga Spring Academy*

Umbrella school. Loga Springs Academy.

https://www.Logaspringsacademy.com

Publishers, S. (2004). *Saxon Math Homeschool: 7/6 (Saxon Math 7/6 Homeschool)* (1st ed.). SAXON PUBLISHERS.

Stranz, D. (2013) *Amazon Book Review for the Learn at Home Series* https://www.amazon.com/gp/customer-reviews/R155HKYHQJYBKE/ref=cm_cr_dp_d_rvw_ttl?ie=UTF8&ASIN=156189513X

V. (2020). *Usborne My First Reading Library 50 Books Set Collection - Read At Home*. Usborne Publishing.

Watts, J. M. (2020). *Writing to Respond: Practice and Assessment: Cultivating Habits of Writing in Grades 3-5 (WRT Workbooks)*. Buddinwriters Academy LLC.

ABOUT THE AUTHORS

 Karen White Porter is a Director of Loga Springs Academy, a former homeschool mom, and a Nationally Board-Certified Teacher. She is also author of the *Emotatude Book Series* that helps people cope with feelings. She taught English, English Language Learning, and English Language Teaching at many American and international schools including: East China Normal University in Shanghai, P.R. China, Hofstra University in Hempstead N.Y., Hillside Public Schools in New Jersey, Saint Andrews University in Saint Andrews Scotland, Belcher Elementary in Clearwater Florida, The University of South Florida, The State University of Florida, and Loga Springs Academy.

She started her own school, Loga Springs Academy in Gainesville, FL, because she wanted to develop a student-centered curriculum. Karen's experience leads her to share her knowledge and expertise in this book.

Dr. Martha Marcella Joseph Watts, affectionately called "Aunty Marcella", is an author, English teacher, teacher trainer, and an independent educational consultant. She is best known for her *Writing to Respond* (WTR) process—an approach for guiding students in writing to respond to what they read. She has published several educational resources to support implementation of the WTR process. These resources include books, workbooks, classroom charts, and student and educator wheels. She is also author of *The Adventures of Iyani* children's fiction series. Dr. Watts has taught on the elementary, secondary, and university levels and has done so in her home country of Dominica, i the US Virgin Islands, and Florida. Her interaction with students in diverse settings gives her the opportunity to observe students' emotional reaction to natural disasters, school unrest, and personal loss in unique ways.

ABOUT THE EDITORS

 Mary Bahr is a nationally board-certified science teacher and field researcher involved in the citizen science movement across the nation. She taught for over 20 years in the Marion County, FL, Public School System and in Ottertail County, MN, for ten years. She served on the State Writer's Committee for the Science Standards for the State of Florida. She brings a deep understanding of science curricula and a love of learning to this project.

Patricia Ashton is an author and the manager of Ashton Biodiversity Research and Preservation Institute (ABRPI). Her books provide the public with groundbreaking research about gopher tortoises, their commensals, and their habitat. She specializes in writing management plans and educational curricula for schools. Additionally, Pat works on plant surveys, habitat monitoring, and habitat management. She also designs risk management, initial suitability assessments, and business plans for preserves.

Patricia has been actively involved in investigating the natural world since 1967, when she worked at Tropical Atlantic Biological Labs on Key Biscayne and explored the Everglades mapping rare plants. She worked on projects throughout Central and South America and the Caribbean as well as in Australia, New Zealand, the Bahamas, Barbados, Spain, China, Western Canada, and the eastern United States. Her work in education, field research, and writing is available at https://ashtonbiodiversity.com/.

K .W. Porter and M. J. Watts

www.ingramcontent.com/pod-product-compliance
Lightning Source LLC
Chambersburg PA
CBHW020037040426
42331CB00031B/674